THE DRIVER'S
LITTLE INSTRUCTION
BOOK

THE DRIVER'S LITTLE INSTRUCTION BOOK

(or What They Don't Teach You in the Highway Code)

Mike Leonard

with cartoons by Bill Stott

Thorsons
An Imprint of HarperCollins*Publishers*

Thorsons
An Imprint of HarperCollins*Publishers*
77–85 Fulham Palace Road,
Hammersmith, London W6 8JB
1160 Battery Street,
San Francisco, California 94111–1213

Published by Thorsons 1995
3 5 7 9 10 8 6 4

Mike Leonard asserts the moral right to
be identified as the author of this work

A catalogue record for this book is available from the British Library

ISBN 0 7225 3163 X

Printed and bound in Great Britain by
Caledonian International Book Manufacturing, Glasgow

Introduction

I'm not a good driver – but I'm trying to be.

I've never owned a car and I didn't discover what a fan belt was until I became a 30-something.

In the last decade, however, I have driven over 250,000 miles (400,000 kilometres) – that's the equivalent of 10 times round the equator or, if I drove in a straight line away from Earth, I'd be on the dark side of the Moon!

I've had a few prangs, a few scares and ran out of juice a few times.

I've performed acts of complete stupidity for which I am deeply ashamed, and I've exceeded the speed limit occasionally.

I've had the pleasure of sharing the road with lots of skilled, courteous drivers, but never a day goes by without finding myself confronted by ill-mannered, selfish road-users who either revel in their behaviour or seem blissfully unaware of it.

This book is essentially about treating your fellow road-users with respect. It also contains a few practical suggestions – and a hint of humour.

If one person becomes a better driver as a result of reading this book, then that will be an achievement. I feel I have become a better driver just by writing it.

All you ill-mannered, selfish road-users: read this book; I look forward to sharing the road with you when you've changed your ways.

And all you skilled, courteous drivers: read and enjoy this book; I salute you and look forward to meeting you on my next journey!

Acknowledgements

The author would like to thank the following for their advice and inspiration: David Brawn, Sheila Crowley, Jane Graham-Maw, Hugh Grant, Chris Moody, Jimmy and Maureen Strode, Gillian Taylforth, Ian and Amanda Thompson, Mary Tuft and the Thorsons team.

He would also like to thank Anne Spedding for her help and for putting up with his bad driving!

- Learn to drive.

- Enjoy your driving.

- Always face the direction of travel.

- Drive as if every other road-user is an idiot.

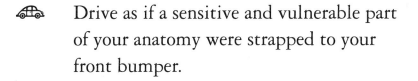 Drive as if a sensitive and vulnerable part of your anatomy were strapped to your front bumper.

Don't encourage anyone to learn to drive against their wishes – driving is not an essential skill.

If you get paid for your driving, drive like a professional.

Don't take driving lessons from your partner or a relative – at the very least it will test the relationship.

- Never let a friend or relative service your vehicle unless they are a competent technician.

- Shoot half-witted drivers with your imaginary gun. It's a great stress reliever and much kinder than the real thing!

Never tell anyone that you are a good driver – an unsolicited compliment from your passenger is worth much, much more.

If you are getting persistent 'earache' from a back-seat driver, buy a toy steering wheel and present it to them when they next get into your car.

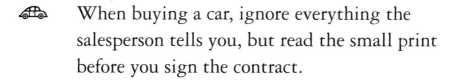 When buying a car, ignore everything the salesperson tells you, but read the small print before you sign the contract.

Don't buy a car just because you like the television commercial.

- Don't buy a car that's the colour of a wet road in bad light.

- Before you choose a particular model, speak to someone who owns one and ask what they think of it.

- Don't buy a vehicle manufactured in a country with a bad human-rights record.

In fading light beware of black cabs lurking in the shadows. They're often the last vehicles to put their lights on.

Signal to other drivers when they have forgotten to put their lights on/off (this also applies to indicators and fog-lamps).

Don't buy a car on the 1st of August.

Refuse the offer of a car if your job doesn't require it. Ask for an increase in salary instead.

Don't try to better your peers by paying to have your company car upgraded.

Never boast about your car to a client or customer.

Don't laugh at drivers of 'inferior' cars. They may be as proud of theirs as you are of yours.

If you're hiring a car for that well-earned break, treat yourself to a top-of-the-range model.

Be especially courteous to drivers of vehicles with foreign number plates.

At least once in your life borrow a soft top and go for a picnic. Even better, once in your life own a soft top and go for lots of picnics.

At least once in your life go for a ride in a Rolls Royce. Even better, once in your life own a Rolls Royce.

Drive with caution near airports and ferryports. The driver in front may have a total of two minutes' driving experience in this country (or be jet-lagged).

Swear liberally at other road-users – it's therapeutic – but remember to check that your windows are closed before you launch your tirade of abuse!

- Never try to outswear a taxi driver.

- Give a wide berth to a car driven by a nun.

- Remember to moderate your language if you have a run-in with a nun!

- Don't be complacent with your driving just because your car has excellent safety features.

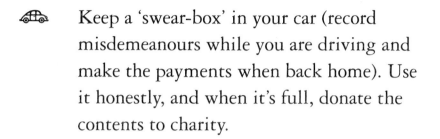

Keep a 'swear-box' in your car (record misdemeanours while you are driving and make the payments when back home). Use it honestly, and when it's full, donate the contents to charity.

Be wary of a car driven by a woman.

Be wary of a car driven by a man.

Never place absolute trust in a set of road markings that allow you to overtake.

In any manoeuvre, give yourself room for error.

Remember that 90 per cent of accidents are caused by human error.

Be especially courteous to elderly drivers.

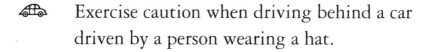 Exercise caution when driving behind a car driven by a person wearing a hat.

Don't buy a car coat. These became obsolete when car heaters were introduced.

Be courteous when overtaking a vehicle driven by someone with a conspicuous set of white knuckles.

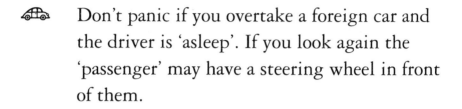 Don't panic if you overtake a foreign car and the driver is 'asleep'. If you look again the 'passenger' may have a steering wheel in front of them.

In slow-moving traffic, leave space for crossing vehicles and additional vehicles.

Take a day's tuition on a skid pan.

Drive like an ice dancer – a symphony of controlled power and elegance.

Don't drive like an ice-hockey player – zigzagging through the opposition at breakneck speed.

- Become an advanced motorist.

- Always acknowledge an act of courtesy by another driver.

- Be courteous to large or slow-moving vehicles, but don't expect courtesy in return.

Write and tell your MP that large or slow-moving vehicles should not be allowed on the roads during rush hour (buses and emergency vehicles excepted).

If you intend to tow a caravan or trailer, choose a suitably powered vehicle; and if possible pull over occasionally to allow faster vehicles to continue at their desired pace.

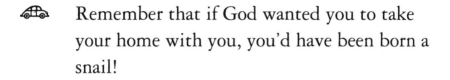 Remember that if God wanted you to take your home with you, you'd have been born a snail!

Avoid travelling in convoy with other caravanners.

At the very least, choose a set of caravan curtains that don't induce nausea in someone driving behind you!

Beware of 'repmobiles' – generally a newish, bland, mid-range car with a jacket hanging behind the driver. Often sales reps have only one thing on their mind – the next appointment!

In a 50-50 situation always give in.
Even if you both give in, you'll have a laugh about it.

If you have a near-miss and it's your fault, make a sign of apology to the other driver – don't just drive away.

Thank pedestrians when they give way to you.

- Never sound your horn in anger at a pedestrian.

- Don't stop at an isolated lay-by after dark, especially if you're alone.

- Never pick up hitchhikers unless you're absolutely confident that you can defend yourself in a nasty situation.

If possible, cycle your usual route once a year. You'll see things you never notice when you're driving, and you'll be reminded just how vulnerable cyclists are.

In good weather, resist the temptation to drive with one arm leaning out of the window. Yes, it may look cool, but one arm redder than the other is decidedly un-cool!

Never boast about how long you've been driving without having an accident.

Expect the unexpected, especially when sharing the road with a taxi.

If you witness a taxi indicating *before* making a manoeuvre, write a letter to *The Times* (only joking – but you know what I mean!).

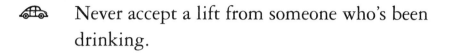 Never accept a lift from someone who's been drinking.

Be extra vigilant if you find yourself sharing the road with a pizza delivery van.

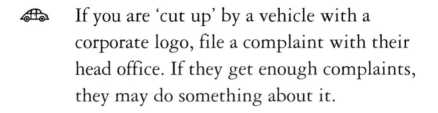

If you are 'cut up' by a vehicle with a corporate logo, file a complaint with their head office. If they get enough complaints, they may do something about it.

Alternatively, if the company produces something you use, boycott the product.

Make a point of not buying a product which is advertised on a billboard being towed along congested roads.

Be extra vigilant when sharing the road with a vehicle that clearly doesn't belong to the driver ('Courtesy Vehicle', 'On Hire From', 'Self Drive', etc.).

Learn to recognize the signs of 'White Van' syndrome (any vehicle exhibiting some or all of these conditions should be treated with extreme caution):

- a white van (usually) with a corporate logo or a name painted on the side
- a set of ladders on the roof
- a front fascia obscured by the contents of an average litter bin plus a

sun-bleached, dog-eared street atlas
- a driver in a woolly hat

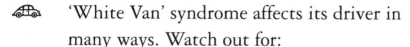 'White Van' syndrome affects its driver in many ways. Watch out for:
- arbitrary use of indicators
- complete disregard for speed limits
- an increase in *their* speed when *you* try to overtake

If there's a 'White Van' behind you, you may be forgiven for thinking that the driver is trying to read *your* speedometer.

On motorways, 'White Vans' often move unexpectedly into the outside lane – and stay there! Their usual location, however, is in the middle lane, regardless of traffic conditions and the speed of the vehicle.

On a positive note, not all vehicles displaying the tell-tale signs of 'White Van' syndrome are driven badly.

A further word of caution: 'White Van' drivers often drive other vehicles!

- Take the red nose/squashed tomato off your vehicle after Comic Relief Day.

- The addition of a spoiler or two may make your car look like Damon Hill's, but be aware that this will also increase your fuel consumption.

- Don't drive in the rush hour, unless you have to.

🚗 Don't take a driving lesson in the rush hour.

🚗 Don't drive on a Bank Holiday, unless you have to.

🚗 Don't drive in London, unless you have to.

Exercise caution when driving behind a car with a couple of cosy cushions on display on the parcel shelf.

If you have the time and the skill, buy a very old car and make it look new again.

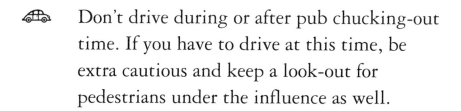

Don't drive during or after pub chucking-out time. If you have to drive at this time, be extra cautious and keep a look-out for pedestrians under the influence as well.

Don't drive with a parcel on your parcel shelf. If you're forced to brake sharply, you may end up with a parcel-shaped dent in the back of your head!

If possible, keep all heavy or potentially hazardous items in the boot, not in the passenger compartment.

If you are without even a modest degree of beauty, don't choose a car to attract sexual partners.

On hot, sunny days, don't be distracted by attractive people displaying their charms. That sneak peek could cost you dearly!

Try sex in a car at least once in your life.

Even better, try sex in a car once a week!

🚗 Or better still, try sex in a car once a day!! (only joking).

🚗 Don't try sex in an MG Midget unless you have the agility of a gymnast!

🚗 Don't try energetic sex in a three-wheeler – you may topple over at a crucial moment! (Did the earth move for you, Darling?)

Try sex and champagne in the back of a stretch limo at least once in your life (make sure the windows and the driver partition have very tinted glass).

Don't try sex in the car when driving.

If you think you're too old for sex, you're probably too old for driving.

If you're advanced in years or in failing health, be honest about your driving ability and be prepared to call it a day.

If your doctor advises you not to drive – don't drive.

Always keep a box of tissues in your vehicle.

Don't try solo sex in your vehicle. Getting caught is even more embarrassing than getting caught with another person!

If you are unattached and sexually active, keep a pack of condoms in your vehicle.

Don't leave mysterious items of underwear in your car.

Remember to wipe the footprints from the inside of your windscreen.

Be wary of a car with football scarves trailing from its windows (especially if yours are a different colour!).

Be aware that your team's colours on display may draw unwelcome attention.

Don't fart in the car, especially if you've got passengers.

Be wary of a car with something tasteless hanging from the rear-view mirror, such as furry dice, a cardboard pine-fragranced tree or a false penis with human features.

Be aware that a car-freshener hanging from your rear-view mirror says to other road-users: 'My car smells'. You're probably also obscuring your view of the near-side pavement, right where a child could run into your path.

 Don't pick your nose when you're driving.

When driving in the country, don't automatically blame your passenger for a sudden bad smell. The increasing use of organic farming methods often creates a distinctive rustic fragrance!

Close your windows and sunroof as you approach a chemical plant or oil refinery.

Beware of a vehicle driven by somebody with a 1980s footballer's hairstyle.

Don't smoke in the car – you'll get a double dose and smell like an ashtray.

If you must smoke, never light up using matches. A detached flaring match-head can cause a disaster in a moving vehicle.

Don't empty the contents of your ashtray onto the ground.

If you see a smoker perpetrate this foul act, don't challenge them (such a person obviously cares very little for this planet and its occupants).

If you feel particularly incensed, record the details and report the incident to the local police. They may not thank you for it but, if there is a case, the driver will be charged with littering.

If the driver is smoking when you get in a taxi and you object, ask them to refrain.

If you've just quit smoking, fill your ashtray with packets of sugar-free mints or potpourri.

Fit a blind-spot mirror to your side-door mirror.

Be wary of a car with an excessive number of cuddly toys on display.

Be wary of a car with too many stickers in the windows. ('We've been to Stansted', 'My other sticker is funny', 'I've had a shag in Milton Keynes', etc.).

If you must display a sticker on the rear of your vehicle, choose one with BIG LETTERS so that an inquisitive driver does not have to drive too close to read it.

Don't eat or drink anything hot or messy while driving.

Keep your vehicle clean and drive with pride.

If you're too lazy to wash your vehicle, at the very least keep the windows and mirrors clean and scrape the dirt from your lights and number plates and reflectors.

- Once a year treat your car to a professional valet.

- Don't throw litter from your vehicle. Next time you're delayed on the motorway, the lane closures could be because litter patrols are collecting *your* rubbish.

- Try to avoid pot-holes in the road, but don't swerve violently.

If you can avoid it, don't drive over a piece of debris in the road, no matter how harmless it looks.

In traffic, never brake or swerve violently to avoid a collision with a stray cat or dog – the safety of humans always takes priority.

On quiet country roads, *do* try to avoid squashing small animals (and collisions with large animals).

Don't use your screen-wash when your sun-roof is open.

Don't use fog lamps if it's not foggy.

Don't use your screen-wash when there's another car close behind.

Don't antagonize other drivers – they may not be as rational as you.

Signal to other drivers when they've not noticed that their inside lane is vacant, but be careful not to antagonize them.

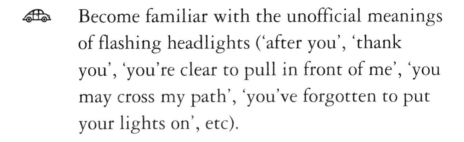

Become familiar with the unofficial meanings of flashing headlights ('after you', 'thank you', 'you're clear to pull in front of me', 'you may cross my path', 'you've forgotten to put your lights on', etc).

Avoid a confrontation with a driver wearing mirror shades.

Use indicators liberally. The more advance information you give out about your intended move, the more chance you've got of surviving it.

When waiting at a junction, leave enough room for another car to pass you on the other side, if possible.

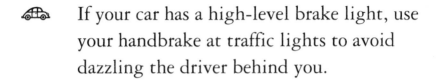

If your car has a high-level brake light, use your handbrake at traffic lights to avoid dazzling the driver behind you.

Beware of a vehicle with its wipers dancing across a dry windscreen. The driver clearly has little idea what is happening outside the vehicle.

Don't leave your windscreen wipers on when it has stopped raining.

Don't read the paper while you are waiting for the lights to change.

If you intend to turn at a junction controlled by traffic lights, indicate as you make your approach, not as the lights change.

If you find yourself at the head of a queue of traffic waiting for lights to change, you are obliged to stay on 'double alert'.

Remember, a green light does not mean 'the road is mine', it means 'proceed if clear'.

If you stall in front of another vehicle, make a sign of apology as you eventually move off.

Give learner drivers as much patience as they need – remember that you were once a beginner too.

Every time *you* drive, treat it as a driving lesson.

Read the Highway Code at least once a year.

Always buy the Highway Code when a new edition is published, then throw the old one away.

Give a copy of this book to someone who's just passed their driving test.

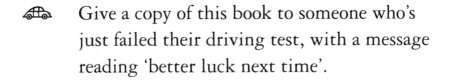 Give a copy of this book to someone who's just failed their driving test, with a message reading 'better luck next time'.

Don't race anyone. A shot of adrenaline may feel good, but it plays havoc with your stress levels.

Always remember, go-faster stripes don't actually make the car go faster!

Write and tell your MP that you don't want more roads and more lanes on the motorway, you want fewer HGVs.

Only wear driving gloves if you are behind the wheel of a Ferrari (or if your heater is broken).

- During school holidays drive with extra caution through residential areas.

- Buy a 'thank you' gift or Christmas card for your child's lollipop lady/man (school crossing patrol).

- Wave to children who wave at you from buses and cars.

Have your car handwashed by the local youth group.

Make your children contribute to the insurance if they're using your car.

When you borrow Dad's car, don't change all his pre-set radio channels!

- Think long and hard before you decide to buy someone a car for their 17th birthday.

- If you see a lone woman stranded on the motorway, inform the police.

- Before you fit a sun-roof or a better stereo, get a mobile phone.

Join a reputable motoring organization (such as the AA or RAC) and keep its number handy.

Keep an ample supply of coins and a phonecard (hidden from view) in your vehicle. You never know when you may have to use a payphone.

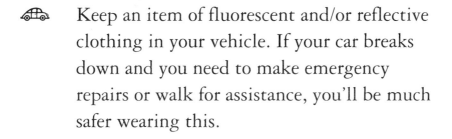 Keep an item of fluorescent and/or reflective clothing in your vehicle. If your car breaks down and you need to make emergency repairs or walk for assistance, you'll be much safer wearing this.

Learn how to change a wheel.

Keep a torch in your glove box.

Keep a notepad and pencil in your glove box.

Keep a cheap camera in your glove box. Use it to record evidence if you have a prang.

Keep a copy of this book in your glove box. Read it when you're stuck in a jam.

- Keep a change of underwear and a toothbrush in your glove box.

- When you buy a car, make sure it's got a large glove box!

- Don't keep a pair of gloves in your glove box.

- Keep a fire-extinguisher in your vehicle.

Keep an up-to-date road atlas in your vehicle (Collins is the Number One). Don't refer to it when you are driving!

Don't buy fuel at a filling station whose incentive schemes have a severely limited life.

Fill up before your gauge hits the reserve zone.

Keep spare fuel in your boot, stored in a substantial container designed for the purpose and clearly marked 'fuel'.

Don't use a hands-on car phone when driving. No phone call is so important that you have to drive dangerously to make it ... and no journey is so important that you can't interrupt it to make or receive a phone call.

- Don't knit when you are a passenger in a moving vehicle.

- Don't shave, comb your hair or fix your make-up while driving.

- Listen to traffic reports before and during your journey.

On long journeys, listen to books on tape.

If you have young children, learn or make up lots of car games and songs.

Never take-in the view when you are driving.

Don't drive to a beauty spot and then stay in the car, no matter how foul the weather is.

Be kind to traffic wardens. Someone somewhere thinks they do a wonderful job.

If you intend to speed, make sure you've got a woman in labour with you.

Don't call the traffic policeman 'son', just because he looks as young as yours!

- Don't leave a £20 note in your driving licence 'by mistake'.

- Think positively – even speed cameras run out of film.

- Attach a sprig of holly to your vehicle at Christmas.

When you visit the Highlands, buy a piece of 'lucky' heather and stick it in your vehicle grille.

Always double-check parking restrictions.

If you think it's cool to flout parking restrictions, think how cool you'll look when your vehicle has been wheel-clamped.

Have your music loud if you must, but remember to dip the volume or close your windows when you stop near other people (be particularly aware of this if you like to sing along).

Don't listen to the 'The Chain' by Fleetwood Mac when driving (it's the theme music to the BBC's Formula 1 coverage).

Listen to 'Jessica' by the Allman Brothers' Band and imagine you're behind the wheel of a supercar (it's the theme music to the BBC's 'Top Gear').

Be aware of the damage you may be doing to your hearing if you play your music too loudly in your vehicle. I SAID BE AWARE OF THE DAMAGE YOU MAY BE DOING TO YOUR HEARING IF YOU PLAY YOUR MUSIC TOO LOUDLY IN YOUR VEHICLE!!

If possible, remove your roof-rack/roof-box if you don't intend to use it within the next week (wind resistance increases fuel consumption).

Keep a photograph of every car you've ever owned. Now and again look back and laugh (or sigh).

Don't leave your car parked near a scrapyard for too long – you might make it nervous!

Always follow directional arrows in car parks.

In a manned car park, park in a space near the attendant's booth, if possible.

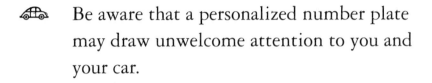 Be aware that a personalized number plate may draw unwelcome attention to you and your car.

Don't automatically blame the driver of a badly parked car. He or she may have been forced to park badly by the action of a selfish earlier parker.

Don't leave the car park entrance ticket in your vehicle.

Take the trouble to park straight in car parks. Next time you enter a car park, it could be *you* who can't find a place because the space created by a badly parked car is too narrow.

If you aren't disabled, don't use a disabled badge or park in a disabled space – apart from the obvious, you may be tempting fate.

Don't park in a space marked 'Reserved for the Chief Executive' – unless you *are* the Chief Executive.

Park away from the herd in car parks. You'll reduce the risk of having your doors dented, plus the walk will do you good.

Don't park next to an old banger in a car park. Chances are the owner doesn't care whose doors get dented.

Park next to or between two expensive cars.

Keep a supply of coins in the car (hidden from view) to pay for parking and for the hire of shopping trolleys.

Take the pay-and-display ticket off your window before you drive away from the car park.

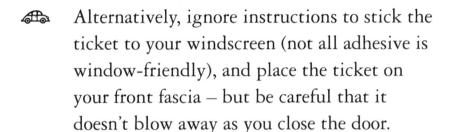 Alternatively, ignore instructions to stick the ticket to your windscreen (not all adhesive is window-friendly), and place the ticket on your front fascia – but be careful that it doesn't blow away as you close the door.

Be wary of a car being driven with a vast collection of pay-and-display tickets stuck to its windows.

If you're shopping for perishable groceries or frozen food in hot weather, take a cool box with you.

When you've finished with your trolley, always return it to the trolley park. Next time you shop, it could be you who has to move a discarded trolley before you can park.

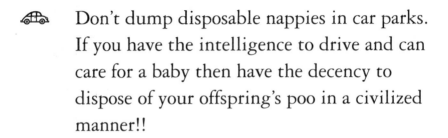

Don't dump disposable nappies in car parks. If you have the intelligence to drive and can care for a baby then have the decency to dispose of your offspring's poo in a civilized manner!!

Avoid vehicles with vinyl seats (unless you are kinky). Vinyl seats, hot weather and bare legs make an uncomfortable combination!

Don't leave your dog in the car in hot weather.

If possible, keep your dog segregated from the passenger compartment. A panicking dog in a moving vehicle is definitely not man's best friend!

When parking on a hill, leave your vehicle in gear with your wheels turned into the kerb.

When using 'nose-to-tail' on-street parking, park near the next vehicle or at the extremity of the designated area. Additional vehicles can then park in the remaining space.

If you park at the extremity and leave a half-car gap behind or in front of you, then one less vehicle can park on the street – next time it could be you!

Ask a passenger to get out of the car to help you park – use the 'hands apart = space till contact' technique.

After dark, park in a well-lit area or close to a police station.

Be familiar with the sound of your vehicle alarm.

When ordering a taxi after hours, insist that the driver doesn't honk their horn to announce their arrival.

When you're leaving friends after hours, don't shout 'thanks for a lovely evening!' at the top of your voice and then drive off, tooting your horn.

Take the trouble to investigate when you hear a vehicle alarm.

Make as little noise as possible when closing your vehicle doors in a built-up area after hours.

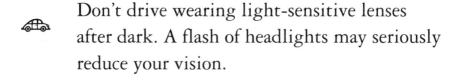 Don't drive wearing light-sensitive lenses after dark. A flash of headlights may seriously reduce your vision.

Keep a spare car key in your wallet or purse.

When driving, always remember 'it is better to be late in this world than to be early in the next'.

I trust you found something of interest in my little book. If you think there is something I have overlooked, write to me c/o Thorsons, HarperCollins*Publishers,* 77-85 Fulham Palace Road, Hammersmith, London W6 8JB. If your suggestion is published in a sequel, I'll give you an acknowledgement.

Happy Driving!